Speed Reading For Beginners:

How to Increase Your Reading and Comprehension Speed and Start to Read Faster

By

Dale Blake

Table of Contents

Introduction 5

Chapter 1. It Is All About The Speed and Comprehension.... 6

Chapter 2. Pitfalls to Avoid 9

Chapter 3. Simple Ways of Improving Your Reading Skills and Comprehension.. 15

Chapter 4. Improving Reading Speed - A Practical Approach 22

Conclusion.. 27

Thank You Page... 28

Speed Reading For Beginners: How to Increase Your Reading and Comprehension Speed and Start to Read Faster

By Dale Blake

© Copyright 2015 Dale Blake

Reproduction or translation of any part of this work beyond that permitted by section 107 or 108 of the 1976 United States Copyright Act without permission of the copyright owner is unlawful. Requests for permission or further information should be addressed to the author.

This publication is designed to provide accurate and authoritative information in regard to the subject matter covered. This work is sold with the understanding that the publisher is not engaged in rendering legal, accounting, or other professional services. If legal advice or other expert assistance is required, the services of a competent professional person should be sought.

First Published, 2015

Printed in the United States of America

Introduction

Speed reading has been a skill peddled by experts putting it on the spotlight. The claim is that speed readers can read up to 1000- 1700 words in a minute while the average person reads 200 to 400 words. The only way to understand if these claims are true is by looking at the different techniques used in speed reading. Only then can we differentiate fact from myth.

Regardless of how truthful or false these values can be, upping your own game in reading will definitely make you a more productive individual. On average, we read hundreds of documents in a day. Add instructions and adverts to this and you get the number of things read in a day to an astounding number. It could be easy to say that a better part of our day is spent reading something, or perhaps trying to read it. Increasing on your reading efficiency will not only make you spend lesser time in the process but also ensure that you do more in a day without necessarily tiring yourself.

Chapter 1. It Is All About The Speed and Comprehension

Reading is an interesting mechanical process only if you factor in the time spent thinking through complex and unfamiliar concepts, which is something that most people reading for pleasure fail to do. You look at a word for several seconds in a process known as fixation, which takes about .25 seconds. Moving your eyes to the next set of words, which is known as saccade, takes about one .1 second on average and it is done once or twice before pausing to comprehend the content you just read. The comprehension process takes roughly 0.3 to 0.5 seconds. When these seconds are added up together, you end up with an average reading speed of about 200-400 words per minute for most college students.

The claim by most speed-readers is that they shorten the fixation period by cutting down on sub vocalization thus a faster rate than the mentioned 0.3-0.5 seconds cut. Speed-reading is an idea that has been around since 1950s but has gone through revival in the recent past due to the development of apps and other technology advancements.

A tip that seems to work for speed-readers is the fact that they stop saying the words in their heads. When reading people tend to subconsciously hear the words in their minds. The claim to faster reading therefore rides on the ability of the reader to break this habit and increase his or her reading speeds by double or triple the previous seeds. A tip that works for most speed-readers is to preoccupy their mouths thus resisting the temptation of reading out the words. When the brain is disengaged from speech, it will be able to tap into your conscious awareness rather than when it is slowed down by when it tries to figure out the meaning of the word.

This is one of the most illustrious things that sets human beings aside from any artificial intelligence implementation. We do not have to understand every word in a text to find out what a sentence means. We do understand text and speech better by doing inference. Applying this concept to your reading will cut down on the total number of words you have to read per unit time without watering down your comprehension power.

One method that works for speed-readers effectively is their ability to skim through content and skipping the unimportant parts. This method does not necessarily teach you how to read faster but rather how to skip content.

Meta guiding is the second speed-reading technique used in the olden days. This requires you to use a pen or pointer to guide through specific words. The point here is to reduce destruction and focus on the specific words thus decreasing your reading speed.

The other method pushes you to read multiple lines and automatically increase your reading speeds. The method that uses this technique relies on expanding peripheral vision and trains readers to focus on more than anything else. In most digital systems, rapid visual representation is what makes it possible for readers to concentrate on a single word as the words flash past on the screen. Speed-reading is possible and necessary but only valid or relevant when you understand what you are reading in the first place.

Chapter 2. Pitfalls to Avoid

Speed-reading can be a challenge if you do not know how to go about it. Usually, most people make certain mistakes when reading which costs them their speed. Once you start learning to speed-read, make sure you avoid several mistakes and reap the academic or professional benefits of doing so. The following eight mistakes when avoided will improve your reading and comprehension skills while enhancing your reading speeds.

Treating all words equally

The first mistake most people make is reading every word at the same speed. This mistake is hard to avoid especially when reading using a word-guided technique say using a pointer or hand to guide the eyes. This means that readers have to go line by line with similar speeds for all the words as if they are following a specific rhythm.

This makes no sense since not everything is equally important. There are sentences and paragraphs that are more important than others are hence are the need to read others at a faster speed. The only way that a speed-reader can be more effective is adjusting his or her reading to the situation at hand.

It is important to adjust your speed based on the material type. Speed u of the easy materials like those found in magazines and slow down on technical content that needs to be comprehended deeply. In addition, if you have a familiarity with the content you are reading then you must push yourself to read faster. You should also adjust your speed based on the purpose of reading. You may not have to read very slowly if your purpose is to get the basic concepts of the read. You need to push yourself through material of this nature although a lot of detail may make your vision blurry hence the need to slow down.

Re-reading

The second mistake made by a majority of individuals is going back to re-read a text when they do not have to. All of us go back to a context at some point although we do not have to. Never go back to reading a single sentence even though you never comprehended it. Chances are that things will become clearer as you continue reading the text. Sometimes, not until you read the entire paragraph will you understand the sentence that is giving you problems. Just like a movie that you did not comprehend at first, you need to continue reading and figure things out at a later stage. The only time you should go back to re-read is when even after reading an entire paragraph you are unable to comprehend it. After all, the important thing is to understand the text.

With poor concentration, chances are that you will be unable to faster since reading requires focus. Poor concentration will destroy your ability to comprehend regardless of you reading it slow or even fast. Generally, the better concentration you have the faster your reading speeds get. You can have the help you need with some techniques in maintaining the focus you need to read faster. First, you can use your hand to guide your eyes across the lines. The second technique that works is eliminating distractions that you can control and focus on reading.

Focusing on speed

The other mistake that costs readers speed is too much focus on the speed aspect. Speed is essential when you start out reading as a beginner but comprehension should be the focus. When you get comfortable with the reading your mind will be able to adjust with the speeds.

Avoid focusing on the mechanics only as this is another common mistake people make. The eyes are mechanical as they allow you to read while the brain interprets and allows for content comprehension. Too many speed-reading programs focus on the eye and forget the function of the brain, which is the most important, is without comprehension the read is void. Beware which program you invest your time and money in.

Being rigid

Most readers make the mistake of holding back when they should be flexible. The only way to master speed-reading is to perceive print in different ways as opposed to staying rigid to the only type of print you were introduced to. The fact that a reader wants to understand at the same rate that he or she did when being introduced to speed-reading is a holdup in its own. These speeds should improve with time as the reader becomes familiar.

Inconsistent efforts and giving up too early are other factors that hinder speed –readers from progressing as well. Learning to master speed-reading skills is a lifelong skill that is easily learnable but the reader must maintain the same excitement all through. Try not to expect instant gratitude if your results are to last. Speed-reading takes time but is definitely rewarding when you are patient enough.

Trying too hard to understand

Sometimes, understanding is never about how much you can remember after a pass on the content. Comprehension reading, as a matter of fact, emphasizes on skimming before reading again if the content you are dealing with is complex enough to warrant a second look. The essence of reading any material is getting the information you are interested in. Doing a first skim lets you know whether the material has that information or it doesn't. If it does, this will also let you know what part of the material to lay more emphasis on.

By using this approach, you can clock a faster average reading speed since you will skim through 'useless' sections faster and take more time soaking in the information at important sections of the document. The most notable thing about this approach is that it does not work on its own. You have to use it in conjunction with other speed reading tricks if you are to achieve optimal results.

Chapter 3. Simple Ways of Improving Your Reading Skills and Comprehension

Improving reading comprehension skills helps a reader to connect better with the ideas on a page and apply it to what they know. The reading is of little value if they do not know anything about it. It is difficult for a reader to retain much if he or she is clueless about the subject. On the contrary, the maintenance capacity increases if the reader has an interest in the subject of discussion. A good example is when a sports fan finds it easy to read sports content because his or her mind can comprehend retain and store this information without being forced to do so. These people can identify relevant type of writings to their interest and will make sense out of it without necessarily working hard at it. They are able to anticipate what will come next in the process.

Even though speed-reading is a technique that must be mastered it is even more crucial to understand and fully comprehend the text that you are reading. Reading is and should be about getting information. It is not about the number of words you are able to read per second but rather about the value, you get from the words. This is explains why comprehension of a text is very important. You need to create a mental framework that helps process the words and ideas. All it takes for one to read fast and productively is a little bit of practice.

Improving your skills in compressive reading calls for motivation, mental frameworks that can hold these information and good study techniques. It is possible to broaden you background of information by reading newspapers, magazines and books as well as becoming interested in the ongoing of the world. These skills will help in better communication as people can construct or make paragraphs from the beginning to the need. This means that good readers are definitely going to be great writers as well. In giving an overview you will see it in the first sentence that will help a framework relevant. When the reader is able to identify what the author tries to project, they will be able to think for themselves thus making them anticipate for more of what the author is writing. When it is positive, the author will succeed in reinforcing the reader's basic understanding and if wrong, the adjustments can be made quickly. The following tips should come in handy for any person whose goal is to read and understand without wasting time.

Pre-read surveys

All speed-reading courses recommended that a pre-reading survey be conducted. The aim of doing this is to gain better understanding of the content and material structure. It is amazing how people can read an entire book only to realize that they have not accessed the content they have been looking for in the first place. Pre-reading will make your reading more effective and efficient by creating a mental gap.

You should start by reading the table of content and the first page introductions before anything else. The next thing will be to flip through the content reading the titles, headings and bold face prints. This is important for a general impression and you should not be concerned about remembering anything specific. This should take no more than five minutes as your aim is to know the layout of the book and location of different topics so that you will know where to go in case you interested is in a specific section.

The next thing to do will be to define your purpose for reading. With a general grasp of content within reach, the next important thing to do is to define its purpose. You need to know what information you expect to gain from reading the text in question. Only when you get to it do you realize how difficult it is to define. Different readers of the some content can have drastically different objectives. Failure to define the purpose will result in ignoring crucial sections and concentrating on unimportant ones such that by the end of the read you rarely understand what actually happened.

However, when you define what you intend to gain from the read you will be able to separate the important from the irrelevant and as such allocate your attention accordingly. You need to be as specific as possible if you want to increase your understanding in a specific area. For this reason you will find yourself asking several question among them being what the author intended you to start doing, what the author expect you to stop doing. Your immediate action when you put the book down after completing it, are there any projects you need to implement once you are done with the book and if how you can apply the knowledge form the book for the betterment of your situation.

Try to create question that the read should answer as you proceed with your reading. Writing down specific questions will help you read with a goal in mind. This is the best way to measure your comprehension since you will notice the answers to your questions as you proceed with the read. These questions will serve as mental cues. The moment you spot a keyword in the text you will be able to relate it to it and your mind will be triggered to start finding answers.

Take note and if possible highlight important concepts

One of the surest ways to embed something in your mind is to write it down. You need to make a note of the important things you read in a text on a separate piece of paper. You can also use a highlighter inside the margin to point out some of the things that really spoke to you. This is the easiest way to remember what you read and make important sections easy to read and review whenever you have to.

Make a post reading review

The final stage of comprehensive reading is determining the lessons you have gained from the read. You need to know if you have achieved your goal or if you have answered, any of the questions you had previously to a satisfactory level. In case you are unable to answer the questions you had before you are supposed to go back to the text for reference. This process will solidify your knowledge in mind and give you a better recall power. With reviews, you will know what you learned, what you did not and whether there is something deeper in the text you need to go into, or find extra reference to comprehend it.

Comprehension of reading is a goal that most people strive to achieve. For the most educated building, a strong vocabulary is a lifetime project that they must undertake. The best way to improve one's vocabulary is to read regularly and make use of the dictionary often. If it calls for it, walk around with a pocket dictionary that you can use to look up new phrases and words. If this is not an option, keeping a list of vocabulary to be looked up later is the best move. Reading books that have challenging texts also help in improving a person's vocabulary. Vocalize the words especially those that are more challenging as this will help you get a mental picture. For a better understanding though, make sure that you read the book several times while highlighting and summarizing the most important ideas. There is nothing a person will not do to ensure that his or her reading is not in vain.

Chapter 4. Improving Reading Speed - A Practical Approach

There is a lot you could do with more time in your hands if you are able to compete reading a text a text in less time than expected. This is achievable only with the right reading speeds. Increasing speed is a process that involves controlling finer motor movement and nothing else. Different approaches have been advanced on how this can be achieved but we are going to look at the most practical techniques.

You need to start by understanding the basic principles of how human visual system operates if you are to reduce the inefficiencies and increase speed and increasing retention capacity. For this exercise to work you, need a page with more than 200 pages, a pen and a timer or stopwatch. The session's activities should be completed within 20 minutes.

For the reading process to work you must minimize the number and duration of fixations per line to increase reading speeds. Most people do not read in a line but rather in saccadic movements with each of these movements having a temporary snapshot of the text within your focus area. With every fixation, each has ¼ to ½ seconds lasting. This can be demonstrating by closing an eye and scanning horizontally in line with your eye thus giving you a feel of distinct and separate movements and periods of fixations.

The next thing is to back skipping and the regression should be eliminating if you are to increase your reading speed by any chance. An untrained reader engages in conscious re-reading and skipping it back which is something that can take up to 30% of your reading time. This is likely to slow you down.

In order to increase the vision span and the registered words in every fixation in horizontal peripheral then use the drills conditioning. You can use the focusing central when it comes to subject's untrained but when in reading it should not be horizontal peripheral vision. This means that they have to forgo 50% of their words on fixation.

To successfully increase your speeds you need to learn the technique, learn how to apply these techniques with speed through conditioning and learn how to test your own reading comprehension. When learning about speed focus first on mastering the motor, control skills and worry about comprehension later. You will need to practice the technique of speed reading and comprehending which is known as the adaptive sequence several times before you figure things out. During practice, you may have to work on getting three times the speed in order to attain your ultimate target speed. There are two techniques that can be used namely the trackers and pacers while the second one is the perceptual expansion.

Common speed reading myths that actually slow you down

Have ever seen someone read a text and thought to yourself how you cannot read a text that fast? Some people tend to be natural fast readers while others stumble on the content as long as they are able to get the information and get it done with. Has it ever occurred to you how some people manage to read texts at super speed and yet seem to understand just fine? Well there could be many reasons to explain all these things but it is important to differentiate fact from myth. There is a high likelihood that you will be held back by a myth and remain at the same place instead of progressing.

The first speed-reading myth is the assumption that reading every letter of a text makes you a better reader. While some people believe that reading every word in a text is what makes you a better reader, what this succeeds in doing is to slow you down. There may be no difference between you and the person who skips irrelevant words, as you will both comprehend what the text. It is possible not to read every word in a text and still comprehend what the author was trying to communicate.

Myth number two that can pull you down is the belief that reading slowly can make you comprehend better. Most people mistakenly think that you can concentrate better when you read slowly. There is no truth in this claim because concentration is not a matter of willpower but reading at an appropriate speed. You are not likely to concentrate any better when reading slowly and instead could be more distracted by the slow speed in addition to wasting time. A good comparison is when watching a movie in slow motion; this is not only boring but also distracting. With proper practice, you will be able to read texts in a group of words rather than per word. This will reduce the time spent on fixation and enhance your understanding because you are will not be distracted.

The other common myth that can slow you down if not demystified is the belief that reading faster interferes with your understanding. Nothing could be far from the truth. Comprehension of texts depends on whether you will be able to retain information after you have read it. Some people read fast while others read slowly. The comprehension differs and it is not unlikely to find a person reading slowly and grasping nothing but the speed-reader having better comprehension. Furthermore, there is scientific proof that speed-reading can improve comprehension of texts. In the end the decision at which speed to read at is a personal decision. Choose what you are comfortable with.

Conclusion

Working with speed-reading training tests is a perfect way to handling the job. If you do not have the time for tests, you could settle to applying the speed-reading techniques to any content you go through. Next time you are reading, instead of trying to soak in each word, take some time and read phrases rather than words. Try to avoid reading in a retrogressive way. Sometimes, you needn't time yourself to identify an increase in performance. If you feel you are faster at reading, then you must be.

With so much material to read in a day, developing good reading techniques is inevitable. Understanding how to create a perfect mix between speed and comprehension will make the entire speed-reading concept more viable. As long as you do not want to enter the Guinness Book, you can settle with a modest balance of comprehension and speed, a balance that makes you a more effective and productive person.

Thank You Page

I want to personally thank you for reading my book. I hope you found information in this book useful and I would be very grateful if you could leave your honest review about this book. I certainly want to thank you in advance for doing this.

If you have the time, you can check my other books too.

www.ingramcontent.com/pod-product-compliance
Lightning Source LLC
LaVergne TN
LVHW021748060526
838200LV00052B/3543